SWIFT THE RIVER HOOSIE

James N West

Swift The River Hoosie, Copyright © 2019,
James N West. All rights reserved.
No part of this book may be used or reproduced in any manner whatsoever without written permission of the author, except in the case of limited quotation in the context of reviews.
All illustrations copyright © 2019 Juli Ann Polise, licensed to James N West for his exclusive use
in any context related to this publication.

All inquiries to:
James N West
Skiff Mountain Press
346 East Shore Drive, Whitmore Lake, Michigan 48189
www.skiffmountainpress.com
jnwest@gmail.com

Interior, Cover Design and Illustrations: Juli Ann Polise
www.juliannpolise.com

ISBN: 978-1-7343912-0-6

Library of Congress Control Number: 2019920063

To my parents Mary and Sam
and my brother Sam

CONTENTS

In The Beginning

Lyrically

Infatuational

Two Tributes

Wits and Twizzles

Episodes

In The Beginning

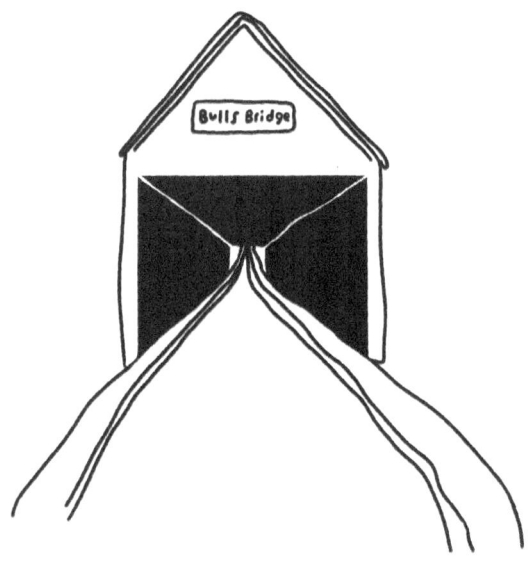

1959

As my hometown faded in the distance
unmoved to say goodbye
loving what I wasn't yet missing
conceived within a sigh

SWIFT THE RIVER HOOSIE

1998

The canopy of trees hid much on Numeral Rock, visible only to eyes that scaled the heights. The boulders, wearing old makeup of lichen and moss, were undisturbed. Gusts of wind lifted the scent of leaf and pine needle decay from the sponge-soft ground, cushioned by decades of trees shedding their temporary disguises. The breeze curled as the sun drenched the air and blazed patches of exposed ground. Inhibitions absconded, allowing instinct to become the art in the moment.

Void of hesitation, allure persuaded an effortless passage, triggering an instant, involuntary shudder. Without distinction between the mountain and myself, the connection was mysteriously cathected. Favorable change had come. These mountains, presiding above this valley, extracted an unspoken pact, existing for as long as I could remember. I was gifted with a way back home. The hills, with their rise and fall into the valley, were distinctly robust. Joined to the mysterious beauty in the life of this land, Kent was like a vicarious lover. It clutched the thoroughfare basins of brook and river, conduits for the life-giving flow of water. It held the soil and rocks and stood vigilant as the passing sky and change of seasons came and went. It possessed the imagination of the many who passed through and those who settled and made a life.

Kent, my hallowed home, impervious to its existence in my mind, spun a lifetime of countless reflections that levied both anguish and exhilaration by its mere existence.

SWIFT THE RIVER HOOSIE

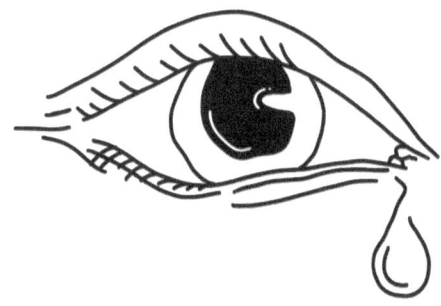

REUNION

Did you perceive
within the eve
of time
to the garden returned
minds joined to restore
ancient memories and lore
healing laughter with spirit discerned

Did time disappear
joy re-appear
collapsing all sense of space
love's gentle employ
gave rise to the joy
souls joined once again embrace

Were we wanting and sad
or open and glad
when a tear filled the well of an eye
if sad we lament
if glad our intent
will make peace at our center reside

In peace would we deem
the end of the dream
awaken to walk this direction
the paths we have known
invite the way home
to the garden at one with perfection

SWIFT THE RIVER HOOSIE

JAMES N WEST

Lyrically

SWIFT THE RIVER HOOSIE

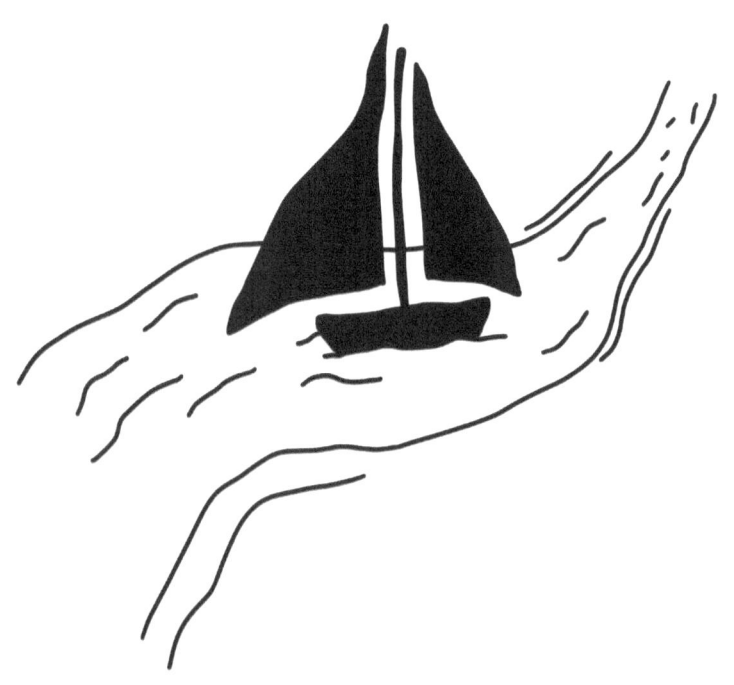

ELEMENTAL

In carbon of clay I stand
Vertical rock walking the round
Powerful magnetic and beautiful
So fragile the element of ground

I form a Lake from inland
Of waves motion or still make gain
Watch lake effect precipitate its promise
To waken the gathering rain

Full circle points all I encompass
Breath from unseen to send
Liquid veil volted fury or the calm
And my sail journeys fair every bend

Of fusion or friction's potential
Kindled brilliant by spark will ignite
The alchemy to render and purify
This I to a pillar of light

In fields among legends reflect thoughts
From silence comes vision sown deep
In the harvest I yield from purpose
Barren heart tilled open replete

SWIFT THE RIVER HOOSIE

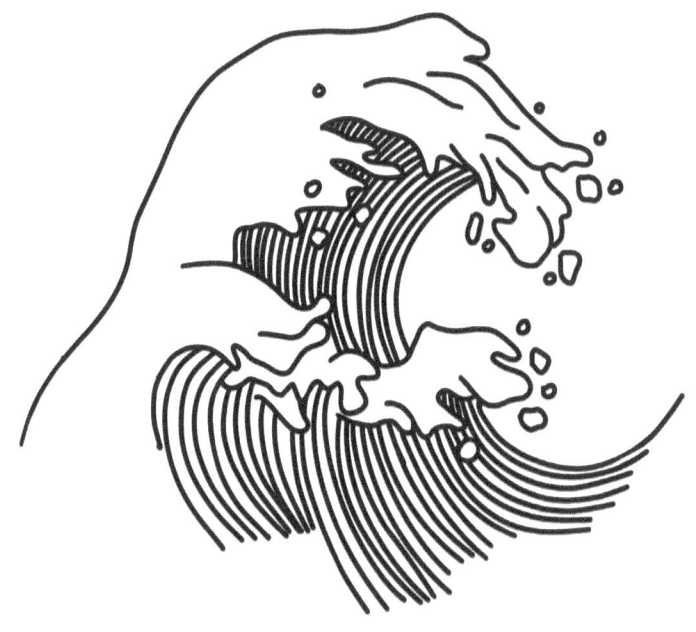

BENEATH THE WAVE

calm
serene
still
undisturbed
rippled
gentle
quiet
unheard

Rough water mounting
deliberate motion
white capped turmoil
rolling ocean
swells of energy
seas that tower
tempest fury
measured awe
with power

Though the waves of change
for a while may define
changeless form of water
the constant through time
symbol of renewal
in the wave or the calm
unaltered by appearance
water's spirit purest balm

Waters of the sea
waters of the lake
water from the river
from the tears of an ache
from love's joy
quenching land
or a thirst and to bathe
water for the soul
beneath the calm and the wave

DREAM TIME: ORIGINAL

Open your dreams
to the night at hand
sleep softly snuggle sweet
while you play in dream land

Close your eyes upon your pillow
in your room my little one
take your rest child of God
'til the darkness is done

Then awaken to the day
after dark will light come
to the promise of the morning
and the new gentle dawn

For we are kept in the care
of the dream while asleep
from night's slumber awaken
from the Dream Time deep

This poem's adaptation is the basis for the children's book, Dream Time, copyright © 2002 and © 2018. James N West

SWIFT THE RIVER HOOSIE

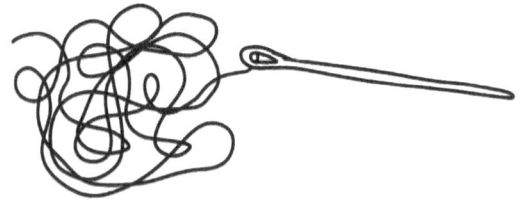

THE CAUSE

Delicate swift
the invisible knife
excised decaying
emotional strife
ends the pall
banned forever
past and present
sewn together
cleared of grief
renewed to waking
opens the road
this path in making

That time in life
a wound it made
effluent release
too long delayed
for want of joy
a heart did bleed
love the cause
love the need

SWIFT THE RIVER HOOSIE

BROOK IN THE GLEN

My heart like a wave runs deep within me
within the shores of my life where I seem to be
will I gather myself and my heart once again
and be with my love near the brook in the glen

Asked my beloved when affections first fell
and in her reply voice inflections did tell
twice upon winter and notable a day
weathered conditions keep harbored vessels at bay

Said I Let's make good any fault and perfect
delayed pleasures of our fathers and mothers circumspect
bone weavers flesh makers upon the lap of our gods
did teach us to grin with their thrill approved nods

We did without knowing and bonded together
their little creations for a time not forever
memory of myself once known then forgot
my purpose their wishes predestined my lot

Then she asked from whence our affections first fell
to my dawdled love these thoughts I did tell
beloved I can sense you're of a great distance
a presence of something afar in the instance

Was it fear of leaving the sway of the clan
of bloodlines lost had you nurtured your plan
or would you lose yourself if we became one
could it be you've been lost since you were quite young

Letting go of the myths though you conceive it untrue
blind sight fades from insights found deep within you
for we were born to creation as God's child upon earth
a life gifted with loving forgiven by rebirth

My heart like a wave ran adrift aimlessly
from the shore I've been cast to the ways of the sea
I recall faded memories of you now and then
of times I would dream of the brook in the glen

Though I miss fragrant words bestowed sweetly to me
remembering the days of love's grand majesty
but like lovers in bliss lost in the splendor
lost in perplexity and the vanishing grandeur

Were they real or imagined mistaken mad passions
consuming ourselves self-inflicted assassins
without song or the dance to make merry be
as though truth was contrived conceived now to be free

And my heart like a wave crashed away endlessly
tumbling walls holding fast muddled aged misery
upon sleeves torrents fell nulling pretension
washed with the muse by the brook in the glen

This moment foretold in the stars by a gypsy
a new day will emerge and fulfill a life destiny
so I spoke with a sage with myself and the Son
and realized in an instant a new world had begun

What's been gained from the loss a fortune of ways
myself and my words and my place in these days
blessed to awaken on love's summit completely
rendered realization revived God given clarity

As a heart aroused opens in waves majestically
within the shores of this life with every complexity
able to gather with resolve once again
will immerse with the muse by the brook in the glen

OUT OF SLEEP

Lyrical genius
flecked with poetic exploits
is the awakening of the muse to stir brilliance

When aroused
it showers the dreamer in a creative fever
then settles to a reflective pool

Skimmed of irrelevance
indelible expressions
course down
hand
to pen
to paper

Strung with allure
words begin to flow
quenching
like a stream
like a river

SWIFT THE RIVER HOOSIE

JAMES N WEST

infatuational

IMAGINATION

You, of imagination
best friend whichever road we go
walk with me to the end
holding hands one day
holding hearts the next

You, of imagination
finest laughter humor can bring
tell that one to me again
silly and shy one day
laughing to tears the next

You, of imagination
painting desire upon my face
color everything in hues red
kiss on the cheek one day
kiss from the deep the next

You, of imagination
feelings spoken fluent from the heart
form every word with passion
conjugate verbs one day
contemplate verse the next

You, of imagination
dream for a time draws nigh
fill the void at any distance
making friends one day
making love the next

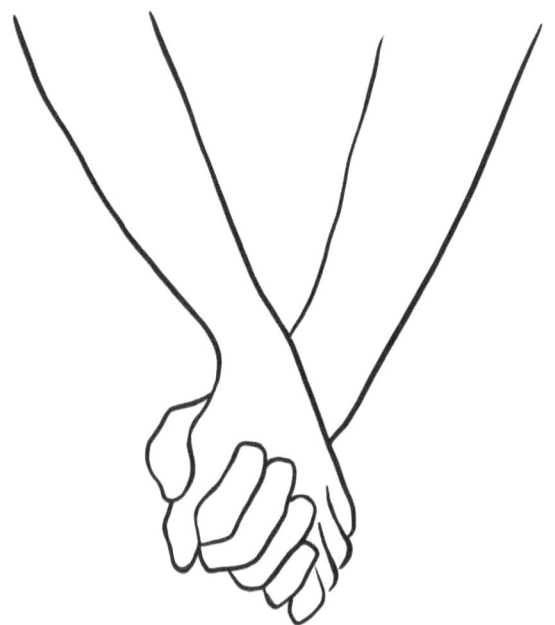

IRRESISTIBLE

Within these have I found
a sense of your presence
by the lake in the moon
with the wind and the sun
longing to be the sky

Longing to surrender
secrets we remember
thought lost in the days
obscured by the haze
of these memories

Irresistible gifts
could I you
resist
falling deep
into these waters

The moon at midday
lover in waiting
peering at me in reflection
as the sun and the wind
form their duet
to soothe as if they were you

Irresistible gifts
could I you
resist
falling deep
into these waters

Today we clasp hands
adrift on a dream
a ship once denied
hope and chance now revive
that our secrets may fall
to the deep as one
awakened in the dream
of renewal

Irresistible gifts
could I you
resist
falling deep
into these waters

BE IT KNOWN

Be it known that I love you
my voice sings about you
I sing out so freely
I love you completely

Be it known that I love you
my voice sings about you
I sing out so freely
I love you profoundly

What's this feeling inside
can't contain will not hide
won't deny the depths that I feel
this love that's so rare yet so real

Be it known that I love you
my voice sings about you
I sing out so freely
I love you completely

My thoughts of the deep are with you
one heart beating for two
two souls that have fused into one
love born of the past has begun

Be it known that I love you
my voice sings about you
I sing out so freely
I love you completely

I will not leave love you so
you've opened me don't let this go
you're a gift I accept what you choose
knowing you means I've nothing to lose

SWEETEST FALL

Sun slows the warm
wind sends the cool
swirling hints
autumn pulls me to you

Like a leaf
released falls
to find earth's
hallowed ground
resting upon the other

As the ground
rises up
to catch his
love's fall
gently
they receive one another

In nature
they complete
love's longing
autumn's suite
fair beauty
came around
in due season

They have given
on love's ground
with each other
to lie down
joined together
in loving
completion

Sweetest fall
in the rise
of autumn

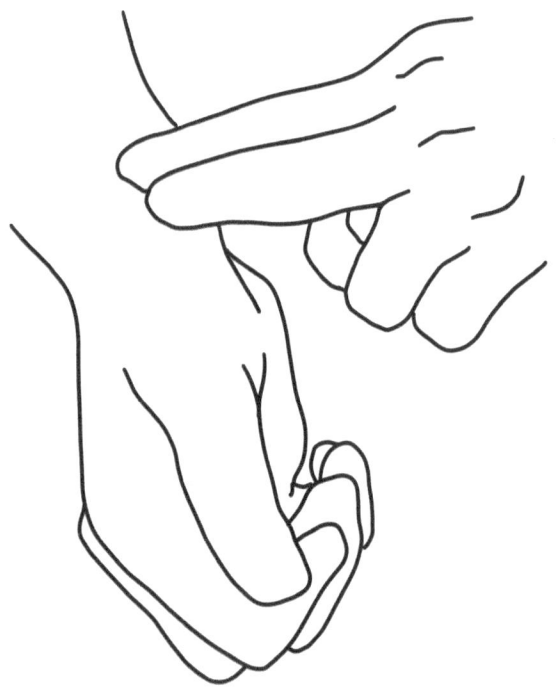

PULSED

You luminesce
in a living room
on a sofa as you rest

I turn my thoughts
from a lower place
a distant faceless contest

Two fingers
touch the flesh of your wrist
ride the cadence
of delicate beats

Another man
discoursing elegance
looking on as he entreats

His observation
to exposed affections
pulsing yet incomplete

In a living room
from a living dream
elusively we meet

A LESSER FAITH

In a jigsaw puzzle will I fit into place
a game board piece moving about this space
cards without faces shuffling slow
will we speak once again it was so long ago

What we made that day
was an oath of devotion
to bond by our blood
a ceremonial notion

We both gave consent
our resolve on a dare
from each other a drop
of lifeforce did share

Time swept us apart
I can still picture your face
sad comes along easy
a flash flood in this place

Meditations of you
fetching phantom of will
did fade with play days
from early years on the hill

In our youth came a shadow
lengthened too soon
eclipsed by our mothers
dark side of the moon

Finding holes in our sun
broken bits of daylight
watch how the beams dimmed
adolescent dreams bright

In a jigsaw puzzle will I fit into place
a game board piece moving about this space
cards without faces shuffling slow
will we speak once again it was so long ago

In our center an emptiness
the stench of buried grief
difficult days of our childhood
send long rains of relief

Drifters on earth
with fortunes to ponder
fair gains to recover
sullied loss if we squander

A simple wish of good will
pleasures held in the mild
our journey our destiny
inner healing a child

This glance at ourselves
a brief time with each other
a look at the likeness
from our ordinary mothers

We once did connect
effortless talks about
our youth and our past
now you've moved into doubt

I called many times
left messages to call
months waiting to hear
I heard nothing at all

As I stare at the present
you vanish in thin air
if I mattered at all
you'd make effort to care

In a jigsaw puzzle will I fit into place
a game board piece moving about this space
cards without faces shuffling slow
will we speak once again it was so long ago

SWIFT THE RIVER HOOSIE

DÉJÀ VU

A gaze
a split second
when first we met

Lit ablaze
a raging fire
in a sensate net

Time flipped
then suspended
each passing moment

Charmed
by your presence
the hour scuttled went

When you left
absence fueled
a sensual quivering

We've rehearsed
from our past
the present delivering

A keen memory
aware
I have known some other you

Incredible
phenomenal
déjà vu

SWIFT THE RIVER HOOSIE

JAMES N WEST

Two Tributes

SWIFT THE RIVER HOOSIE

The Schaghticoke Indian Tribe (SIT) is a small reservation in Kent, Connecticut, located across Macedonia Brook about half a mile from The Kent School heading south on Schaghticoke Road, or off Route 7, heading north on Schaghticoke Road from Bulls Bridge. A fellow classmate back then lived on the reservation and attended Kent Center School in the village. Although I did not know her well, 40 years later, I wrote the following tribute and after an arduous search, was able to locate and talk with her on the phone for about an hour. We shared humorous and what turned out to be, insightful stories from our youth. The Schagticoke, as their name by definition suggests, settled near the confluence of two waterways. In this instance, the Housatonic River and Ten Mile River. We often rode our Schwinn bicycles to the reservation entry on Schagticoke Road, recalling at age seven a senseless fear, influenced by Hollywood's depiction of our relationship with Native Americans. It was delightful and refreshing to talk with her, discovering a friendship that did not exist prior.

SWIFT THE RIVER HOOSIE

CONFLUENCE

Who are you Chicky Strever
and where did your people go
refresh my memory refresh my eyes
undo the fear of childhood lies

We rode Schwinn stallions to reservation point
imaginations filled with the weapons of fear
wondered when arrows would fly our way
then we flew with the wind in our hair

Formless lies the arrow in the quiver of ignorance
shapes the fear we cleverly hide
two sides of a stream can form beauty
alone we remain on the divide

Your memory reminds perhaps not all
in the valley were aware of you though
a friend of yours from the Kent School Tribe
beyond the prejudice in friendship tried

To bridge the stream to share the waters
a gesture to gently compel
a return to help us reconcile
the youth we knew so well

But the Schaghticoke without a presence
like a flower's fragrance wanes
we can only recall from memory
the truth that now remains

An elusive intrigue about Chicky's land
puzzled a dream of wonderment
two waters gave birth to a confluence
two worlds were set apart within Kent

SWIFT THE RIVER HOOSIE

David Armstrong was a gifted and well-known watercolor artist from Kent, Connecticut. David, his brother Kip and I spent many hours fishing the known waterways around Kent. They placed me under their wing and were like adoptive older brothers. Kip, David and their sister Mary grew up at Kimadee Hill, the home built by their father, William H Armstrong, author of the book Sounder. Kimadee is an acronym taken from the names of the three children. It was a place where faculty families from Kent School were invited to enjoy swimming and the simplicity of easy conversation. I visited David at Kimadee shortly before he passed away in 1998. The tribute that follows is from our visit that August day.

SWIFT THE RIVER HOOSIE

KIMADEE

On Kimadee Hill we sat for one hour
as the day to the evening did pass
you offered a toast iced tea and a cheer
to each other we raised a glass

And the air was so good
so easy to breathe
we remembered the garden of peace
Kimadee

We fished Choggam brook
every pond stream a river
Housatonic Macedonia
the names we remember

From the river to the hill
Housatonic's endless rush
over rocks carries up
water's sound healing hush

And the bells of the sheep
clap not on the hill
hang by their stall
I can hear even still

And the air was so good
so easy to breathe
we remembered the garden of peace
Kimadee

SWIFT THE RIVER HOOSIE

That day at the pool
open well in the land
where I knelt stirred a blessing
for you from my hand

The blessing was given
and we I believe
through your life in your art
are the ones who receive

From your hand gifted vision
in the colors and the light
forms the beauty brilliant treasures
waking senses through your sight

And the love we remember
through your legacy
springs from the garden of peace
Kimadee

JAMES N WEST

Wits and Twizzles

SWIFT THE RIVER HOOSIE

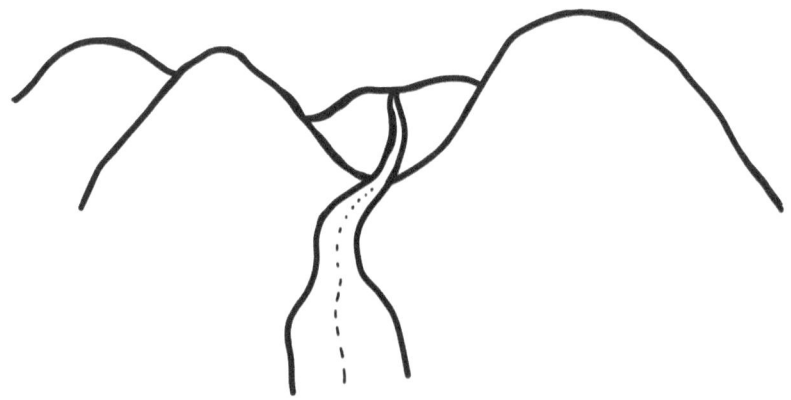

JOURNEY

Destinations hastily engaged overlook the relevance of the road

Embrace the journey
for clarity and purpose are meant to be gained along the way

AtOneMent

no goal
just be

no past
set free

FOLLY

Void of wisdom
choices are fraught with pain

WRITE INSIGHT

Writing is an art
to convey a story

editing is the desired insight
to reform the writing

ABNORMALLY NORMAL

Normal
is something
other than the experience
of self-pitied victims or pretentious fools

REFINEMENT

The fortitude to endure grief
comes by means of grace and measures of hope

SWIFT THE RIVER HOOSIE

OUTCOME

Persistent admiration for other approval
in truth
will kill the relation

SWIFT THE RIVER HOOSIE

CHEMISTRY

Affectionate attraction
attracts like affection

SWIFT THE RIVER HOOSIE

INNOCENT

Naive intentions oft bear misgivings

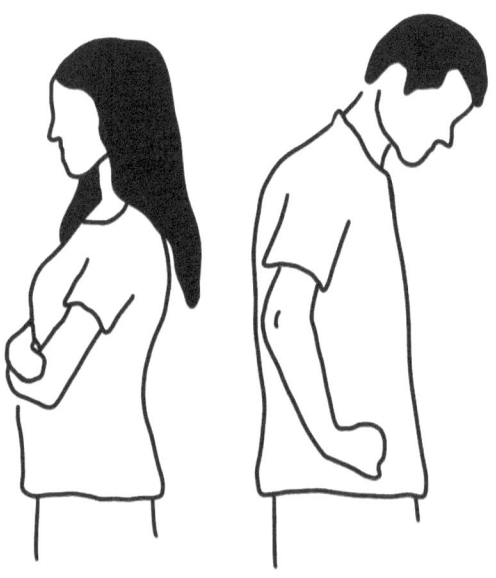

'TIL DEATH DO US PART

When prolonged silence
infects a relationship

indifference
silently invites the demise

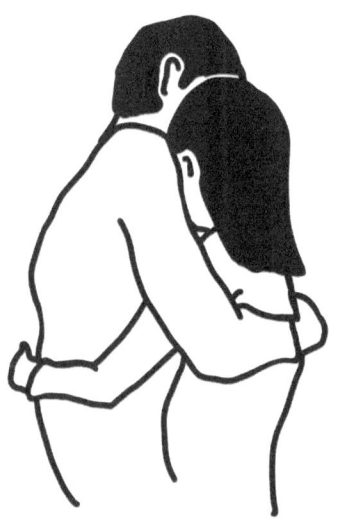

COMMITMENT

Relationships
live or perish
by the proportion of will
to engage

SWIFT THE RIVER HOOSIE

WHERE SHADOWS FALL

In death
a shadow casts
upon those that loved

A death
within the heart
casts its shadow
upon one

FOR EVERYONE

Had the world more beauty
would my eyes see clear
through a heart
which worships
its wonder
thoughts fill with the warm
from a shiver
when I
realize
in the world
we're together

SWIFT THE RIVER HOOSIE

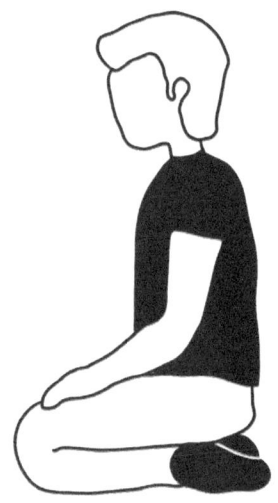

WHEN WE KNEEL

Perplexed by matters held in the heart
time ticks with uncertainty
with each passing tock
Christ will reveal
dissolving the block
from a
humbled spirit
willing
to be taught

SWIFT THE RIVER HOOSIE

GRACE

This universe
abundant well
vast beyond the veil
gives mysterious
secrets rich
when unknowing
we avail

RESTRUCTURE

Just as there are no limits
to the number of revisions
you can impose
on the structure of a sentence
there are no limits
to the number of times
you can restructure
Your Story

PURPOSE

Upon things that you dwell
insights from your well
while dreaming or tending a thought
as you think
so you are
as you reflect raise the bar
make clear your intent
to be sought

eureka!

HUNCHES

Can we know
beyond a guess
suspend the doubt
favor yes
that we can
come to know
things untold

Thoughts of no
gains nothing new
thoughts of yes
to knowing's true
gives a glimpse
before we knew
what's disclosed

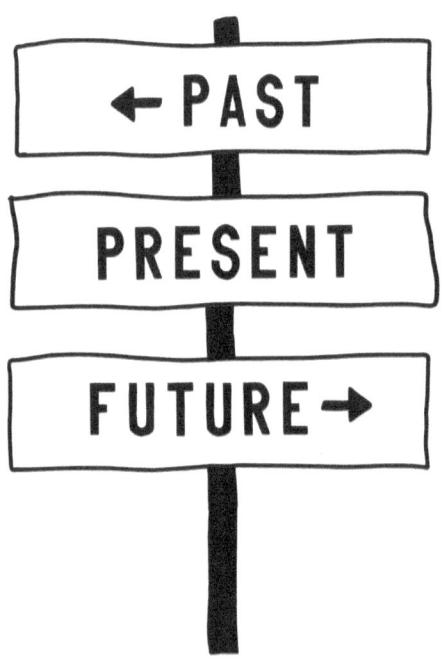

NOW THE PAST FORTHCOMING

Today
while reflecting
the past on my mind
as the day slipped away
to a future awaiting
each now moment
passed me
by

OBVIOUSLY HIDDEN

I know simple thinking
behind a thought
will likely in you spawn
intellect I say
can never outthink
the superior brilliance
of brawn

(Ignorance is bliss)

FORTUNES

As a fortune at the end of a Chinese meal
cannot foretell happiness
so too
fortunes accrued in life
cannot promise contentment

RECONCILIATION

No matter what preceded
no matter what has been done
when asked with sincerity
Christ will reform
the fault in our flesh

your treasure is inside. Keep looking.

ESSENTIAL ESSENCE

By its existence a reunion took place
joined to the gathering
emotions made haste
in waves
came the essential
God given grace

As connections reopened
joy couldn't hide
revealed the true essence
it was always
inside

RIVER LIFFEY

It was the day before
on the day before
no strolling the shores of Liffey
no water swells
nor distant bells
from the steeple upon the cliffy

but what I heard
a single word
she came to call
for Jimmy

I pondered within
with a widening grin
did she know just how
it did me

it spilled from her lips
this endearing slip
her affections
pronouncing Jimmy

a spark in me lit
more than a wee little bit
for in the moment
she stands here with me

I could think it much more
far from the shore
when she called me
her one-time Jimmy

I'm a chancer you see
but I might as well be
on the banks
of the River Liffey

THE JUST TWO POSITIONS

A note of discontent
that being not from you
rather the void of place and time
where we are not

Were we found together
where is that place
and when in time
will it be so

Settle close to me
suspend the query
allow reason a place
beside a reclaimed youth

Headstrong thought
dissects fair bestowals
plays the mind
miscues the heart

Overrule the head
incite the ways
of a fruitful cause
let fondness stir again

Seek the place
of a rose blossomed voice
null the rising juxtaposition
comes to wither our song

Raise the flag
above the kingdom of the heart
and let these words hail
the emergence of destiny
alas to decree

Nobilities have made
noble laws trappings laid
to place law above love
court of the fool

True love will abide
though the world seeks to hide
from the truth
love needs no earthen rule

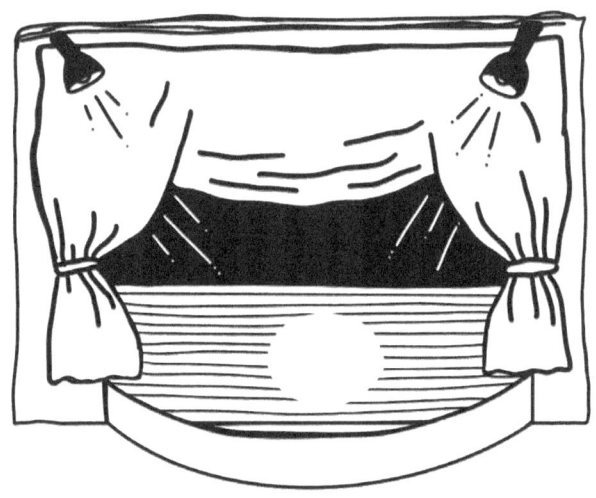

WAITS FOR NO FOOL

What has he done with his timepiece
the moment
misplaced where he was
raging the call
of the curtain
called to passion
not the act
as it were

The moment misplaced
onward rages
sensing fraud
a facade
to display
from his wares
that are worn
from waiting
must still adorn
as his part
in the play

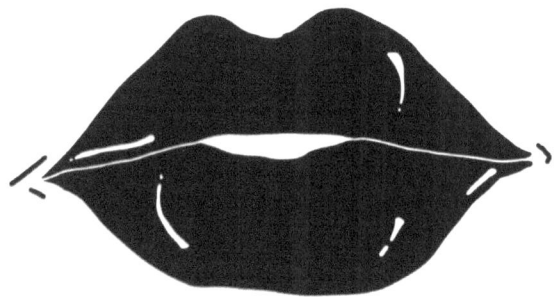

GG

When no lips press
no tongues collide
no physical incursion
swapped in kind
sweet encounters
can have lasting ties
for things unseen
before our eyes

SWIFT THE RIVER HOOSIE

TWODOM

Ricochet cow
thrown by Samson
from wall to wall
sans sound
come giggles
from the warrior
of twodom
when cow-plastic
thuds to the ground

SWIFT THE RIVER HOOSIE

JAMES N WEST

Episodes

SWIFT THE RIVER HOOSIE

IN THE MOMENT

Standing in line, the conversations from seated customers droned softly throughout the coffee bar. Passively observing, the baristas tinkered and brewed behind the counter. There was one, a fair "emissary of extraction" who gave away plentiful smiles and graced the understated decor of the café. Wearing casual attire, her sweater drooped askew below the left shoulder; yanked up on the right. She was attractive with particular physical attributes that drew attention to the ordinary. For a moment, I forgot why I was there until my turn to order was at hand. Greeted by her full grin, I refused to justify any action toward flirtation, aware of the wide gulf between our respective ages. "A Grande, dark roast, please." After completing the transaction and taking the cup, I sat and sipped. As the coffee was cooling, I became amused and simultaneously startled, any relationship ambition would be challenging at this stage and age of nearly seventy years. I recently read again about Low-T; the silent, creeping nemesis of aging males. Stealing another brief look toward her, my mind admired the youth before my eyes and I momentarily longed to be back in my mid-twenties. As I was reflecting, an image of myself came to mind and leaned straight at me as if to say: don't get your hopes up.

OPENING

"Who opened you up?" Sitting with my brother in the exam room at his doctor's office, this physician was new to us both, one of over two hundred cardiologists in the group. Dozens of sub-specialties: adult, pediatrics, interventionists, non-invasive, invasive, women's health, electrophysiologists and so forth. He asked me if I was a physician. My brother mentioned at the onset that I suffered a heart attack recently, which I quickly added, "It was a STEMI; 100% blockage of the LAD," which meant an ST-segment Elevation, Myocardial Infarction, with complete blockage of the Left Anterior Descending artery (known as a widow maker) resulting in tissue death of an area in the heart muscle. "Are you a physician?" Not many people would state their diagnostic profile in the manner I did, but I clarified I was a respiratory therapist. He asked again, "Who opened you up?" It was later that afternoon when rethinking his question; it was Christ who opened my heart, it was Dr. Duvernoy who opened my heart's vital artery. Both were miracles.

ONCE UPON A TIME

I just learned of another who committed suicide. Uncomfortably close to the family, far enough from the person to forego grief. Nonetheless, my mood sank thinking about loved ones, thinking about what the individual may have been dealing with. What is it that mentally pushes someone to end their life? Many have had passing thoughts of calling it quits, but to put a gun to the head, to put a rope around the neck, is too much to grasp. I wondered how many, testing their resolve, may have accidentally caused the knot to tighten or unintentionally squeezed the trigger, not really intending to go through with the act. Knowing we all have to die, I tried to put myself in the place of a troubled soul, choosing in that precise moment to be done with mental anguish. I pondered why the connection with life and friends, the love of children, wife, husband or a loved one, would not be enough to vacate the awful decision. How painful and how lonely can it be to lose a sense of purpose or hope?

Humbling one's helplessness to God, to others or the medical community can be immensely difficult. It's understood, vulnerability and weakness are hard to admit. We all have unconditional permission to make that admission. Let someone partner with you to help. Your life is worth living. Find someone to stand with you. A small reason can be noble enough to carry on and allow you to care just enough. For God's sake, for your sake, there are individuals who can embrace you and help you choose to stay.

National Suicide Prevention Lifeline: **1-800-273-8255**
The phone number listed above is provided for general information only and no claim is made regarding its operation, the services intended or the services provided through the National Suicide Prevention Lifeline.

YOUTHENIZED

Respiratory Care became my chosen career by default. For all my early life, I intended to enter seminary and the Episcopal priesthood. As an eight-year-old, I was convinced the priesthood was my destiny, aware of my love of worship, a knack to connect with people and to be a follower of Christ. I was drawn to be like my Dad. I wanted to emulate him. As his son and as an Altar Server, belief in the Gospels and being around the sanctuary felt very much like home. Something happened, subtle and invisible, but impossible to ignore. I had become unworthy, it seemed. The vision to follow my father, grandfather and two uncles toward ordination derailed. As interest in girls developed in 7th grade, puberty altered all of creation. The wonder stirred feelings and brought conflict that increasingly became incompatible with pursuing holy orders. Or so I thought. I didn't talk with my parents about the shift or the waning confidence to serve in a priestly capacity. It became an obsessive issue as sexual thoughts dominated the majority of waking hours, leveraging shame in view of purity. Feeling less than pure, emotional and intellectual conflict undermined direction. Superstitions were at play as well. Healthcare presented an alternate, less holy way to fulfill a calling to serve the sick and suffering. While in high school, guidance counselors arranged a day at the hospital lab which proved to be interesting, but failed to finish well. The introductory experience included observation of dozens of incubating cultures, how they were processed and, quite simply, it caused me to gag. The smell was intolerable. After high school graduation and with some searching, I began and completed paramedic studies but did not pursue licensure. Shortly after, I commenced nursing school to become a nurse anesthetist. Simultaneously, I was allowed to observe surgery at a small hospital and quickly found the operating room undesirable. I switched to Respiratory Care, completing studies and board examinations, launching decades of work as a Respiratory Therapist. Forty years later, I joined The University of Michigan in the homecare medical division, teaching caregivers about complex equipment and caring for people on home ventilators. Each therapist had approximately thirty-five to forty infants, children and adults on their ventilator caseload. The follow-up visits included testing and documenting the function of ventilators, medication delivery and humidification systems, airway clearance and monitoring devices, plus assessing and documenting the patient's health status, medications, breath sounds, oxygen saturation and exhaled carbon dioxide values. On one routine afternoon visit, I was at the home of an infant, proceeding with the protocol. Throughout the visit, the infant's elder, three-year-old chatty sister, had many busy questions. At one point I said, "It's a beautiful day, today." Her reply, "Is it today, already??!" Enchanted, feeling like I was right where I belonged, innocent charm reawakened a grateful sense of career choice, enriching the satisfaction of helping others.

THE RIVER HOOSIE

The Housatonic River, or "Hoosie," runs approximately one hundred fifty miles from western Massachusetts through western Connecticut, spilling into Long Island Sound. I was, we were, fortunate to live beside the constantly streaming river in Kent, Connecticut on the campus of The Kent School where my father was Assistant Headmaster and Chaplain. Kent was a private, Episcopal preparatory school that took its name from the village on the other side of the Hoosie. The village was where we bought basic staples and groceries.

We loaded into the car and drove the short mile from the village grocery, crossing the bridge over the river toward the school campus and home. Turning left at the entrance of the school, Dad drove past the clay tennis courts and the alumni house to the curve at the floodwall, the buffer between the river and the campus dormitories. We eased around the corner of the single-lane, which had just enough room for opposing cars and ran parallel to the river another two-hundred-yards below the wall. As we drove next to the Hoosie, my father asked me to lean up toward the front seat. Easy to do as no seatbelts were available to restrain any bodies in those days. I slid toward the front. He asked to see my hat, which I lifted off my head and handed to him. "How long have you had this," he asked as he rolled down his window. He continued driving slowly and with one swift, frisbee-style motion, he sailed my hat into the river. "Sam! Why did you do that," voiced my mother. My mouth dropped wide open. "We'll get him a new one. It was filthy," was my father's reply. Panicked, I was swimming in my head, straining to see where it landed in the water. Gone! I managed to squeak two words past tight vocal cords, "My hat!" True, it was frayed in places and had smudges of dirt from constant use, but it was part of a daily uniform and unequivocally, the capstone of my identity. Somewhat sympathetically, Dad interjected, "Oh listen, we'll buy you a new one."

    Reflecting back, I believe my father may have felt regret for the sudden toss, perhaps prompted in part by my mother's remark, "You shouldn't have done that, good grief!" Hers was the final word in the moment. I sat quietly for the remainder of the short drive home, infused with the specter of the unexpected. Humiliated, something deeper, more significant, took root that day. I had fished and waded in the waters of the Housatonic on other days, but this day, something metaphysical took place between the river and me. Swift, the river Hoosie became a refuge of contemplation and a steady source of reflective calm.

SWIFT THE RIVER HOOSIE

About the author

James "Jim" West has been writing since 1998, inspired by the love for his beautiful hometown, Kent, Connecticut. The father of four incredible grown sons and two adorable grandchildren, he graduated from Stephen's College, Columbia, Missouri with a degree in healthcare and psychology and is a retired respiratory therapist of forty years. He also taught Tai Chi and meditation classes in southwest Michigan for many years. He currently resides on a lake in southeast Michigan where he continues to write full time. He has authored two children's picture books, a comforting bedtime story, Dream Time, to be published in mid 2020 and an endearing inspirational book, Where Katy Lives, to be published in late 2020.

About the illustrator and designer

Juli Ann Polise is a graphic designer, photographer, illustrator and content creator originally from the New York metro area. She graduated from the University of Michigan with her B.F.A. in art and design, and now resides in Chicago working as a freelance designer and creative with food, travel, and lifestyle clients. She has a passion for traveling, and has been to 20 countries across 6 continents and takes inspiration from the new cultures she experiences to fuel her creative process.

www.ingramcontent.com/pod-product-compliance
Lightning Source LLC
Chambersburg PA
CBHW021114080526
44587CB00010B/512